ELEN C

JONATRONIX

THE SANDS OF DECEPTION

Contents

Birdy's story 2
Chapter 1: The sands of the desert 3
Chapter 2: A safe house? 8
Chapter 3: Safe landing 13
Chapter 4: The pharaoh's trap 18
Chapter 5: Secrets of the pharaohs 24
About the Valley of the Kings 32

Birdy's story

My name is **Birdy**, and I'm from future Earth. 2099 to be precise. My world is at risk – a giant asteroid is on a collision course with the planet.

Kalvin Spearhead, head of **END CO** – the most powerful company on Earth – plans to build a giant vortex machine to send people back in time to escape the asteroid. He has assembled a team of human-like robots, **Tick-Tock Men**, to collect seven **Artefacts of Time**. These Artefacts will be used to power his machine.

My gran, **Professor Martin**, is the head scientist at END CO. She has shown me Spearhead's plans; she doesn't think his machine is capable of transporting vast numbers of people. Even if the machine does work, it will have a devastating effect on history: it could change everything! Gran has tried to tell Spearhead, but he won't listen. I decided I had to try to stop him. I have borrowed one of my gran's old-tech time-travel vortex machines – an **Escape Wheel** – and am trying to reach the Artefacts of Time before the Tick-Tock Men do.

Luckily, I'm not alone on my journey. I've met four new friends – **Max**, **Cat**, **Ant** and **Tiger**. They have special watches that can make them shrink to micro-size … which comes in handy when the Tick-Tock Men try to stop us!

Chapter 1: The sands of the desert

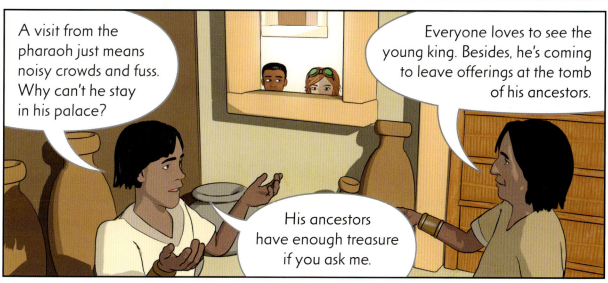

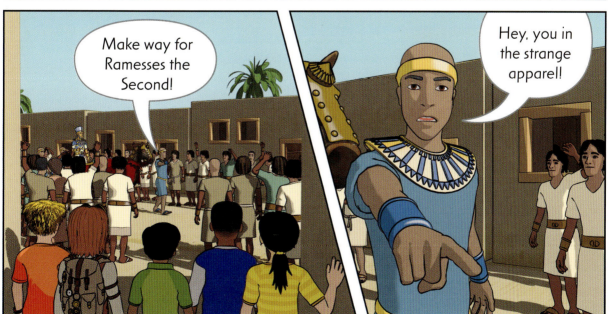

Chapter 2: A safe house?

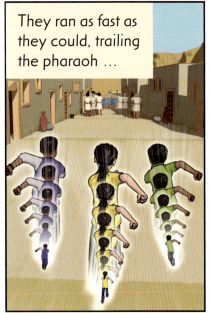

Chapter 3: Safe landing

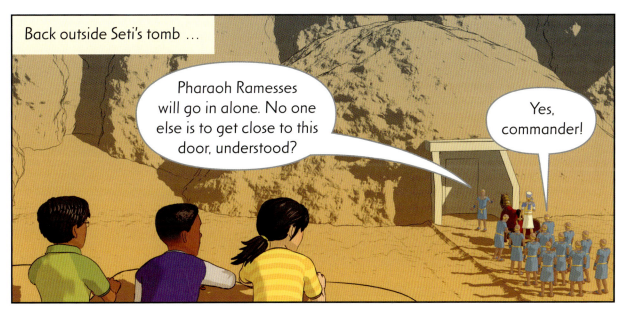

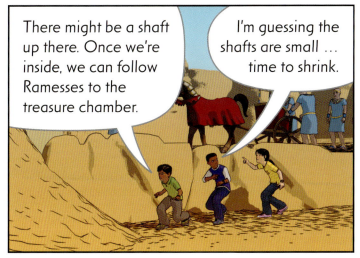

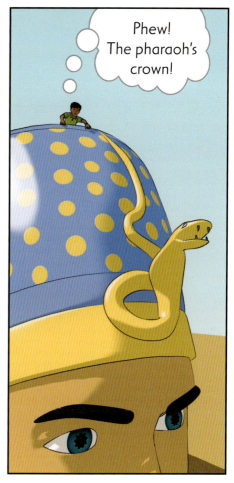

Max and Cat didn't take long to realize what Ant was listening to …

… the pharaoh was a Tick-Tock Man!

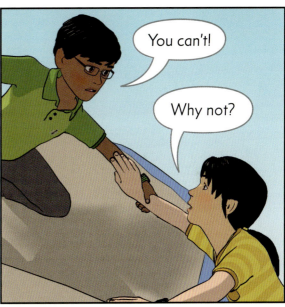
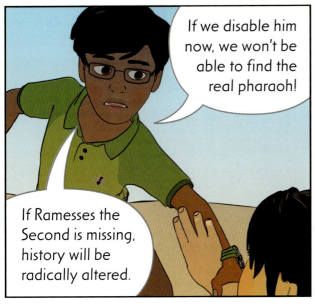

Chapter 4: The pharaoh's trap

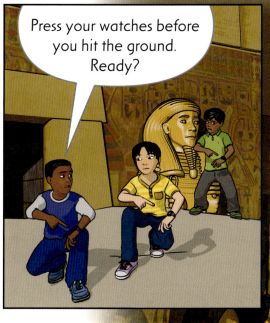

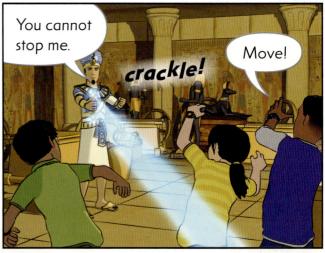

Time Paralysis Weapon

1. Every Tick-Tock Man carries a Time Paralysis Weapon (or TPW for short).

2. When the trigger is pressed, the TPW issues a blast of energy that creates a disturbance in the space-time continuum. Anyone enveloped in the blast is held in freeze frame, frozen in time.

3. The freeze frame duration depends on the height and weight of the victim. A *stun* setting can last anything from fifteen minutes to several hours, but a *restrain* setting can last years.

4. To the person trapped, it seems as though no time at all has passed.

5. A victim can be freed by reversing the freeze frame on the original weapon.

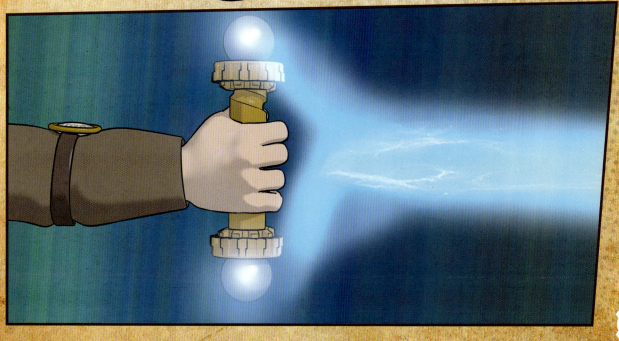

Chapter 5: Secrets of the pharaohs

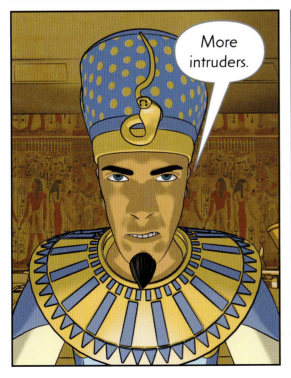

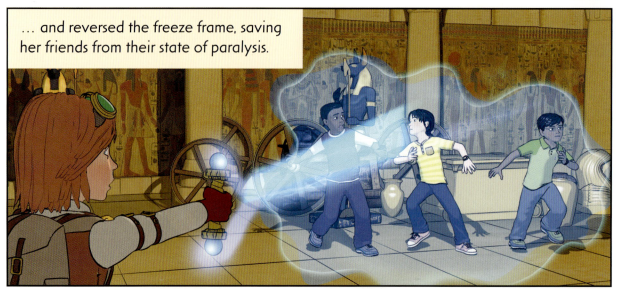

About the Valley of the Kings

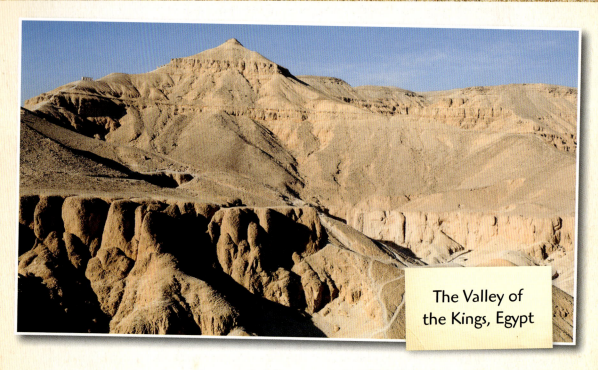

The Valley of the Kings, Egypt

In Ancient Egyptian times, in a period known as the Old Kingdom, pharaohs were buried in impressive pyramids. However, these were easily broken into and the pharaohs' treasures often stolen. Instead, pharaohs of the New Kingdom were buried in complex underground burial chambers in a place called the Valley of the Kings.

The Valley of the Kings was used between the 16th century BC and the 11th century BC. Seti's burial chamber was discovered in 1817 and is one of the most richly decorated tombs in the Valley of the Kings.

Seti's son, Pharaoh Ramesses the Second was one of Egypt's most famous rulers. He was a young man when he became Pharaoh and he ruled his people successfully for nearly 70 years. Ramesses expanded the Egyptian Empire and oversaw a huge building programme. He was so revered as a ruler that he came to be known as Pharaoh Ramesses the Great.

Seti's Sundial was discovered in the desert near the Valley of the Kings by archaeologists in 2013.